An Anti-Prophetic Church

Reconnecting God's Bride With God's Voice Today

Darius K. Walton

Copyright © 2022 by Darius K. Walton.

All rights reserved. This book or any portion thereof may not be reproduced or used in any manner whatsoever without the express written permission of the publisher except for the use of brief quotations in a book review or scholarly journal.

First Printing: 2022

ISBN: 9798849481371

Darius Walton www.dariuswalton.org

Ordering Information:

Special discounts are available on quantity purchases by corporations, associations, educators, and others. For details, contact the Publisher at the email address listed below.

U.S. trade bookstores and wholesalers: Please contact Darius Walton Ministries booking@dariuswalton.org

Chapter One: A Prophetic God

Chapter Two: God's Prophetic Church

Chapter Three: The Anti-Prophetic Church

Chapter Four: Rise of the Real

Chapter Five: Not Just Jezebel

Dedication

I want to dedicate this book to the woman that gave me my introduction to the prophetic, Bishop Carolyn Webb. You were a fearless pioneer willing and ready to speak the future and the mind of God.

I also want to dedicate this book to my spiritual lineage. You all are in my heart daily and I could not be who I am without you.

To my Apostle Carnail Stokes and the entire reformation I serve in, I love you all forever. We are building 21st century saints in real time! Our hour is now!

Foreword

Acts 5:38-39

"Therefore, in the present case I advise you: Leave these men alone! Let them go! For if their purpose or activity is of human origin, it will fail. But if it is from God, you will not be able to stop these men; you will only find yourselves fighting against God."

The response of Apostle Peter in this passage was to inform those in power to refrain from conspiracy talk and plots in efforts to bring the move of God to an END!

Of course, in that day just like ours, anything new is first threatened and sometimes hazed into being. However, this was an attempt to bring an utter end to something ordained by God. The wisdom of the Apostle was to say if it is of men it will come to nothing. But if it is of God then those who oppose it fight God!

For years, many that led the church and have influence to weld her are oftentimes more focused on being right than Spirit led and spiritual. We must rightfully divide the Word but we must also uphold the protocols of the Spirit that is in partnership with the Word! For the letter alone kills but the Spirit brings life.

In this passage men had been taken into holds and counsel was being made as to their wrong and what would be their end. Sometimes in efforts of defining the truth and feeling that we are the truth's protector, we imprison the truth – never discovering what does this truth look like in my current time.

There are times we imprison people because they don't fit within the current definition of our truth. Holding them to what we believe something is because it doesn't fit in our working definition. This doesn't make your truth the truth. This makes your truth a prison. When something is, it is. It will stand throughout time, season, and many understandings.

Simply put, there are many understandings of God that man has said didn't need to be understood anymore. Many functions of God that man has said aren't active anymore! These truths have become the foundation of many! Truths that have shaped cultures, families, perspectives, and hearts. The question is can anything in God die? Does God do things just to end them? Or is there an evolution to all things?

I encourage you with this. Most times where a truth is discovered is not the place where truth is perfected! Many have brought an end to something they just couldn't define for the time they were in. Therefore, what can't be explained has been expelled. However, just as God breathed on the mind of Moses and showed him the beginning, so shall the Lord reveal an old thing in a new time!

Prophet Walton skillfully introduces, defines, and discloses the measure of the prophetic for our current time in this book with great conviction. I believe that he is one of the ones who is anointed to bring great definition to our time!

I encourage anyone to read this rendering in its entirety to ensure full understanding of a gift we so need in our time- the Voice of The Lord!

Don't just read this book. But be open to the truth within it.

Apostle Bishop Carnail Stokes
Father & Founder of The Nation Ministries
& Churches of the Nation
Houston, Tx

Introduction

Before we get into the reason for this book, I must share with you principles that will help provide an understanding of what the prophetic is.

God has a kingdom. His kingdom is the sphere of His rule and sovereignty. When the Pharisees demanded of Jesus that He tell them when the kingdom of God would come, Jesus responded "'The Kingdom of God cometh not with observation:'" (Luke 17:20). Which indicates, that God's kingdom is not something that can be watched with natural eyes. The kingdom of God is a spiritual sphere or realm. It is His actions and attributes. His kingdom is the realm of how He moves and flows. It is a complete domain of His divine decisions.

Whenever or however God moves in the lives of men, it is proof that His kingdom has come. Anytime God decides to heal someone, it is the display of His kingdom (Luke 9:2). When God decides to cast a devil out of someone's soul, mind, and body, it is because His sphere has come (Matthew 12:28). Anytime He decides to speak expressly to those who serve Him, it is a depiction of His realm.

In other words, when we refer to the prophetic as a prophetic realm, it means we are talking about the parts of God's kingdom that He uses to divinely communicate with mankind. God's many functions are simply diverse parts or pieces of His realm, His kingdom.

Therefore, to say that God is prophetic is simply saying that a part of His realm still speaks to men!

One of the Hebrew words for "prophet" is *nabi* which means one who speaks for God or His mouthpiece. In other words, a prophet is God's mouthpiece. A mouthpiece is a thing designed to be put in or against the mouth. Oftentimes, in sports, a mouthpiece is worn as a guard to protect the mouth. For instruments, a mouthpiece is what helps the musician make the appropriate sound on their instrument. With this in mind, today's church must realize that the role and responsibility of a prophet are not to please the ears of men. Real prophets are sent to the earth as agents of God to be His vessel, guard His mouth, and make the sound that He desires to make. The prophet was never designed to live a life of his or her own. The prophet cannot and does not govern his or her own life. It is governed by God and His will!

The word "prophesy" in Hebrew is *naba* which is used to describe the function of a true and authentic prophet as he or she speaks God's message. This means that when a prophet prophesies, it must remain unfiltered and unadulterated. It also means that the prophet's job is not to solely tell you about when you'll get married or what type of car you'll drive. The prophet's prophetic duty is to communicate God's message. Whether it be to an individual or a corporate group of people, God's message must be communicated! God as the sovereign and supreme Spirit knows the lives of His people. He knows every intricate detail about those whom He has created. He knows the number of hairs on your head (Luke 12:7). However, God's main goal is not to convey to you things that you already know about yourself. God's main message is to communicate His plan for your life (Jeremiah 29:11). The prophet's job is to be the vessel that reveals the pages of your life that God has already written out from before time began (Psalms 139:16).

Therefore, the essence of the prophetic is not to wow men or to promote the status of a man or woman. The true essence as to why God has provided the presence of the prophetic realm is because He still wants to speak to those He created.

In today's world, we see a vast amount of those who have abused this realm. They have done things claiming to be prophetic, deceiving men and women. We have seen liars come forth and claim to be prophets, damaging the integrity of the office. But this book has come to you to show you that there are still several thousands of prophets that have not bowed to Baal (1 Kings 19:18). There are still prophets who are pure voices with pure hearts! Yes, the body of Christ has seen the elevation and the promotion of imposters and liars but there is still a remnant that remains! A remnant of people who are mouthpieces for God! We must make sure we do not take on an anti-prophetic attitude and mindset. The office has been abused but don't throw us away!

To desire to eliminate that realm of divine communication is to refuse to speak with the one that made you! For the time that we are in and we are going into, we need the pure voices back! Around 2017-2018 I preached a series of messages entitled "Bring Back the Prophets!" The focus was not to praise the office of the prophet over the other offices that God has given to the church but to raise awareness that even though you've experienced a few false ones, real prophets still do exist! We must bring back the divine communicators as essential voices in our churches worldwide!

Chapter One:

A Prophetic God

When God's kingdom is ready to express itself, He speaks to His servants. God's kingdom is His sphere, it is His realm. It is the place of His divine decisions. God's kingdom is the center of His movement, His actions, and His attributes. Within God's kingdom, there is a protocol He's established when He is ready to move. This protocol is absolutely prophetic. It is established in the book of Amos that God will do absolutely nothing without first revealing it to His servants the prophets (Amos 3:7). God is so prophetic that He ascertains that He includes the prophets in the details of His movement.

The Ruler of this kingdom we are in as believers does not do anything until it's been revealed to His prophets. Now God, the sovereign one, has established this protocol. God makes it clear that His actions are first revealed to His communicators and messengers. This reveals the significance of the prophetic to God and His kingdom. Everything about God is prophetic. Everything God does is prophetic.

The Power of Prophecy

Prophecy is the divine communication of God to man. Prophecy can deal with times (past, present, or future), seasons, positions, instructions, directions, people, places, and even nations.

The greatest misconception of prophecy is that it is merely a prediction. That is how the world defines prophecy. However, if prophecy was merely something as light or unreliable as a prediction, it would not become a law to kill the prophets who prophesied things that did not come to pass (Deuteronomy 18:22). If prophecy was a simple prediction, then whether it came to pass or not wouldn't quite be a big deal. News anchors predict our weather every day and how frustrating it is to be prepared for rain and not see it, or to hear it's going to snow and it is the exact opposite? To reduce the prophetic to being just a prediction is to do a disservice to the certainty of God's voice. When God speaks, it is sure and it is dependable. "For all the promises of God in him are yea, and in him Amen…" (2 Corinthians 1:20). I believe that both written promises (the scriptures) and spoken promises (prophecy) are yea and amen in God!

There isn't anything that God is currently trying to figure out or guess concerning your life. The pages of your life were already written out by God before you were even born (Psalms 139:16). Therefore, God's prophecies can't be aimless guesses for your life. Prophecy is the expression of God's thoughts and His mind concerning an individual, a time, or a nation. Once God says what He is thinking, He leaves it to the believer or listener to align themselves with what He has thought concerning them.

Prophecy has the ability to peek into the mind of the Creator; the very mind of He who is infinite. This is why Paul made it very clear that we "know in part, and we prophesy in part" (1 Corinthians 13:9). The mind of God is too complex for us, being finite beings, to know the totality of His divine mind. Therefore, when we receive His divine messages, it is only a peek into His mind.

It's important to understand that prophecy and the prophetic, in general, is not a new thing in God. It has been something that God has used from the beginning and even concerning the beginning to get His point across. When Moses wrote the book of Genesis, He wrote about a time that he was not even alive to see. That's prophetic! As God was giving Moses the revelation, I can only imagine what must've been going through his mind – but the record of the detailed prophecy of the past is what has shaped our lives and even our ability to hear God speak today!

In this chapter, we are going to first go through biblical examples of prophecy and then I will give some personal examples of how I've seen the power of prophecy flow and operate in today's time.

Prophecy Shifts Seasons

"And it came to pass after many days, that the word of the LORD came to Elijah in the third year, saying, Go, shew thyself unto Ahab; and I will send rain upon the earth."

(1 Kings 18:1)

"And Elijah said unto Ahab, Get thee up, eat and drink; for there is a sound of abundance of rain. So Ahab went up to eat and to drink. And Elijah went up to the top of Carmel; and he cast himself down upon the earth, and put his face between his knees, And said to his servant, Go up now, look toward the sea. And he went up, and looked, and said, There is nothing. And he said, Go again seven times. And it came to pass at the seventh time, that he said, Behold, there ariseth a little cloud out of the sea, like a man's hand. And he said, Go up, say unto Ahab, Prepare thy chariot, and get thee down, that the rain stop thee not. And it came to pass in the mean

while, that the heaven was black with clouds and wind, and there was a great rain. And Ahab rode, and went to Jezreel."

(1 Kings 18:41-45)

Oftentimes in the old testament, you will see that when God would give a prophetic word to a prophet, it would be described as "the word of the Lord came to..." This alone is an indication that prophecy must be received from God. It is not something that comes by way of one's observation, opinion, or rationale. The word of the Lord must come to you. This also reveals why prophecy isn't based on the preferences of the messenger. There is no respect of persons with God (Romans 2:11). Prophecy is not a tool used to build an audience or gain favor with man. The word of the Lord came to Elijah to shift the season of an entire nation.

In 1 Kings 17, Elijah uses his prophetic authority to declare that there will be no rain in Israel. After many days, the Lord speaks to Elijah in 1 Kings 18 that He's decided to end the drought. Elijah now has a prophecy for Ahab that comes with instructions.

In between the time of the prophecy and the manifestation, Elijah has a showdown with the prophets of Baal. Through this, it is proven that God, *Elohim*, is the only true and living God. This alone shows that the purpose of the prophetic is always meant to reveal God and His existence. How many more souls would we win with prophecy if we prophesied with the intent to prove God's existence? In fact, how much greater would we see God use us and trust us with the secrets of men if our goal was to portray and prove God as the only living God? The more God can trust you, the more He'll reveal insight!

Elijah was a man that God could trust. In Elijah's state of depression and suicide (1 Kings 19:4), God still speaks to him and tells him to "... Go, return on thy way..." (verse 15). In Elijah's lowest place emotionally and mentally, He receives yet another prophetic assignment. Elijah was a man that was found in such a place of obedience to God that even in his darkest hour, he was still trusted! Indeed we trust God, but how great it is for God to be able to trust and rely on us for His will to be done in the earth. Are you one that God can trust?

Elijah's prophecy to Ahab shifted the season that the entire nation was in. Prophecy has the ability to speak to current matters of the earth. Once prophecy is placed on that thing, whether it is a person, place, or nation, the supernatural power of God comes upon it. Once God's word is sent, it must accomplish itself "So shall my word be that goeth forth out of my mouth: it shall not return unto me void, but it shall accomplish that which I please, and it shall prosper in the thing whereto I sent it." (Isaiah 55:11). When a word from God comes to a person, place, or nation, it comes with a responsibility to accomplish itself. The power of prophecy causes the natural to align with the supernatural; therefore, causing famines to be turned into an abundance of rain (1 Kings 18:41).

I remember a time in 2017 when the Lord sent a word to a middle-aged woman who I had just met for the first time that shifted her entire season. Unbeknownst to me, she had been on a rather difficult journey regarding the prophetic. She is a prophet but her former pastor was not prophetic and did not believe in the prophetic. Therefore, being in transition, she was looking for a word and teaching that could help her understand who she was as a prophet. Not knowing any of this, as I began to give this woman the word of the Lord before I could even think about it, my mouth said "and the Lord says I'm going to heal you from that pastor that discouraged you in the prophetic"… she screamed and dropped to the floor! After this word, she became a disciple and God really birthed her as a prophet. Authentic prophecy can bring you out of famines into abundance.

Prophecy Interrupts Plans

"And when Samuel saw Saul, the LORD said unto him, Behold the man whom I spake to thee of! this same shall reign over my people. Then Saul drew near to Samuel in the gate, and said, Tell me, I pray thee, where the seer's house is. And Samuel answered Saul, and said, I am the seer: go up before me unto the high place; for ye shall eat with me to day, and to morrow I will let thee go, and will tell thee all that is in thine heart. And as for thine asses that were lost three days ago, set not thy mind on them; for they are found. And on whom is all the desire of Israel? Is it not on thee, and on all thy father's house? And Saul answered and said, Am not I a Benjamite, of the smallest of the tribes of Israel? and my family the least of all the families of the tribe of Benjamin? wherefore then speakest thou so to me?" (1 Samuel 9:17-21)

"Then Samuel took a vial of oil, and poured it upon his head, and kissed him, and said, Is it not because the Lord hath *anointed thee to be captain over his inheritance?"* (1 Samuel 10:1).

Saul has just lost his father's donkeys and is almost in a panic because this has a lot to do with his father's livelihood and business. In an effort to find the lost donkeys, Saul's servant suggests to him that they should inquire of the seer and prophet, Samuel, about where the donkeys were. In those days when man wanted to inquire of God for direction, solutions, and answers, they went to God's mouthpieces (1 Samuel 9:9). When they get to Samuel, he tells Saul that the donkeys have already been found and shifts Saul's focus to what God has said about him.

Saul had a plan in mind, but God had His counsel to release. Indeed, many plans do we have as human beings but it is only the counsel of God that will stand (Proverbs 18:21). The power of true prophecy has the ability to interrupt whatever plans you have devised within your own heart. This must be done in order for us to be set in the trajectory of

God's will. God has a course for all of us to take and these courses can be revealed through prophecy.

The reason why we must take the prophetic more seriously than we ever have before is that the world, not just the church, is in need of real direction. There are pandemics, wars, racial conflicts, religious deceptions, and more that prophets and prophetic people must hear God for. What would happen if the voice in the ear of presidents and kings was a prophetic voice, a voice that spoke on behalf of God Almighty?

Saul receives a prophecy that he feels is so distant from him and his reality. How could God be calling Saul to be a captain of the Lord's inheritance while he felt like he was the very least of his tribe and family? God has a way of speaking things that don't add up naturally.

Many of you have had moments like this. You've received prophecies about your greatness while you felt the smallest. You've received prophecies about your wealth while you felt the poorest. This is because God does not speak according to what we think we deserve based on our current situations. God speaks from eternity. He speaks from a finished place. God knows endings and He specializes in making sure you receive the necessary details to achieve the ending that He's designed (Jeremiah 29:11). Natural knowledge should never be a source for prophecy. People who know people's personal business and mask it as God speaking are liars. Do not misunderstand me. You can prophesy to people you are familiar with. But you must never take what you know or heard about someone and try to disguise it as prophecy. May the fear of the Lord and the spirit of repentance hit those that have done this! It is the operation of flesh (the soulish realm) and carnality. Operations of the flesh and carnality are at enmity with God's Spirit (Romans 8:7). For example, while you may see the present situation or may know a certain individual's past, you cannot prophesy from this carnal understanding, you must give that individual what God thinks about that person (Psalms 139:17). Prophecy is the sum of God's thoughts, His concepts, His will, and plan. If I give you what I think about you and what I think your life will become, this is my prediction, not God's prophecy.

Most of the first encounters I had with those that are now my sons and daughters mirror this Saul and Samuel moment – they received a prophecy that they knew was from God but was so distant from their current realities. Prophecy interrupts man's plans!

I vividly remember one friend calling me to see if he should take this job opportunity that actually allowed him to make more money than he was currently making. He called me excited about the job and the journey it would take him on but then he asked "what is the Lord saying about this job?" Well, I was a supportive friend up until I heard God's response. I immediately heard the Lord say "This is not the door!" So I communicated this and he ultimately stayed at his place of current employment and within a year, the company he was going to shift into ended up shutting down. Man has many plans, but God's counsel will stand!

You have to yield your life to God's prophecy. It will indeed be an interruption and most days it will require you to rely on a strength that is not your own. But that is the beauty of God. He never gives a word that won't accomplish itself! While you live in obedience, His word manifests itself.

Prophecy Does Not Embarrass, It Edifies

And David said unto Nathan, I have sinned against the LORD. And Nathan said unto David, The LORD also hath put away thy sin; thou shalt not die.

2 Samuel 12:13

David finds himself in a place of sin against God when he devises a cunning plan to have a woman's husband killed for his vain benefit. The Lord sends Nathan to give David, the king, the word of the Lord. Prophecy is not just for the "layman", prophecy is for leadership as well! I believe those God has called to be leaders and senior leaders of assignments must remain open to the voice of prophecy in their personal lives as well as their ministry. This must be done because leaders are not exempt from falling into temptations, sins, and grievances against the Holy Spirit.

When Nathan, the prophet, approaches David, the king, he has a word of correction and rebuke from the Lord. However, he does not deliver this prophecy harshly nor dishonorably. Nathan starts by using an allegory that David can relate to. Nathan uses sheep to help David see the error of his ways. This had to have been the wisdom of the Lord in Nathan because this approach affected David in a far greater way than if Nathan had approached him in dishonor and disrespect. May this generation know this kind of wisdom! Yes, correction and rebuke will come to those whose hearts have fallen away from God but it does not mean His love for the fallen one has lifted or expired.

Prophecies should not embarrass, they should edify! Paul gives the prophetic three purposes – edification, exhortation, and comfort (1 Corinthians 14:3). The word edification in Greek is *oikodome* which means the act of building, to build up. I remember a time when my best friend received a "prophetic word" from someone and it left her feeling horrible afterward. She called me and asked me "Was this God?" I responded, "Did you feel built up afterward?" Her answer was no. This is a clear indication that the prophecy did not come from God. When God sends a word, He sends it with enough grace to restore the receiver of the word. Even with a word of correction or rebuke – it should be done with enough love to turn that heart back to God, not the opposite.

David's sin was real. God's anger with the sin was real. But God's love for David was just as real (Acts 13:22). This is why God's response to David's repentance was an immediate reversal of David's death sentence (2 Samuel

12:13). If you are not going to prophesy with the intent to redeem men back to God, you should not prophesy at all.

If you prophesy judgment and take joy in the expectation of God condemning man to Hell, you have what I call "the angry prophet syndrome". The person we see with this in the Bible is Jonah. He gave Nineveh the word of the Lord, the people repented, God changed the judgment, and Jonah got mad! This should not be so if you have the heart of the Father. You should not be angry about God redeeming man.

Prophecy has the power to build up. Most people associate the prophetic with doom and gloom and this is not always the case. I remember in 2018 when everyone was prophesying that America was receiving destruction and was releasing words as if God almost hated America; I went into prayer one day and the Lord said to me "I actually love America. I have a plan for this nation." I wept greatly after hearing this. I wept because we associate the sins of a nation with its destiny when the reality is, if God can redeem Israel time and time again, He can surely redeem America; there just has to be enough voices that are actually speaking the will of God into existence in the earth as it is in Heaven (Luke 11:2).

The focus and goal of releasing prophecies should never be to see how much sin you can expose, it should be how much liberty can you bring to the souls you are being called to.

I remember a time when a middle-aged woman was visiting my father's church where I served at the time. She was of Hispanic descent and it was my first time coming in contact with this particular woman although her family was friends of the ministry. While ministering to this lady I saw a very graphic vision of her being sexually abused. Her cries for help rang loud in the ears of my spirit. It was probably one of the most disturbing revelations I've ever received and I can only imagine how traumatic it was for the precious lady. Being sensitive to this circumstance, I did not state exactly what I saw. The Lord laced my lips with wisdom and I said, " The Lord calls you His daughter. He says you are not a woman without identity. You are not a woman of rape. You are His daughter" The Lord also showed me how there was a lingering shame because of what had been produced from this tragic occasion in her life. As the Lord spoke to me, I told her "The Lord says He's removing the shame from what has come out of this tragedy. And I see a court case that the Lord will grant you favor with. You will not have to fight with it anymore"

    It turned out, that the beautiful pre-teen daughter standing beside her was conceived from this tragedy! Oh, God does indeed give beauty for ashes! Her daughter began to weep and she testified privately that they were in a current battle in court with the offender and that lies were trying to be formed against her at the time. Today, we testify of God's victory for that woman and her daughter!

Although this word was not a word of correction for her, if I delivered the prophecy without wisdom, it could've potentially become an embarrassing moment for this mother and her precious daughter. This is the wisdom of God that Nathan used. Take nothing away from the prophecy, but deliver it with wisdom that it might be received in love by the hearer. Those that flow in prophecy should minister the truth of God in love (Ephesians 4:15). I can't even count how many leaders have consulted me for God's truth concerning themselves and their ministries in private. I don't feel slighted in any way when this is done. I actually enjoy it. I enjoy it when a leader has fallen and come to me because it allows me to extend God's truth in love and mercy. I enjoy it when a leader is having a problem with a certain member and they consult with me about what God's counsel is concerning the matter.

Prophecy should not be played with nor mixed in with one's opinion or personal perspective. Prophecy must be given from the mouth of God with the purpose of edifying God's people.

Prophecy Exposes Unrighteousness and the Unrighteous Decree 13-23

"And the messenger that was gone to call Micaiah spake unto him, saying, Behold now, the words of the prophets declare good unto the king with one mouth: let thy word, I pray thee, be like the word of one of them, and speak that which is good. And Micaiah said, As the Lord liveth, what the Lord saith unto me, that will I speak. So he came to the king. And the king said unto him, Micaiah, shall we go against Ramothgilead to battle, or shall we forbear? And he answered him, Go, and prosper: for the Lord shall deliver it into the hand of the king. And the king said unto him, How many times shall I adjure thee that thou tell me nothing but that which is true in the name of the Lord? And he said, I saw all Israel scattered upon the hills, as sheep that have not a

shepherd: and the Lord said, These have no master: let them return every man to his house in peace. And the king of Israel said unto Jehoshaphat, Did I not tell thee that he would prophesy no good concerning me, but evil? And he said, Hear thou therefore the word of the Lord: I saw the Lord sitting on his throne, and all the host of heaven standing by him on his right hand and on his left. And the Lord said, Who shall persuade Ahab, that he may go up and fall at Ramothgilead? And one said on this manner, and another said on that manner. And there came forth a spirit, and stood before the Lord, and said, I will persuade him. And the Lord said unto him, Wherewith? And he said, I will go forth, and I will be a lying spirit in the mouth of all his prophets. And he said, Thou shalt persuade him, and prevail also: go forth, and do so. Now therefore, behold, the Lord hath put a lying spirit in the mouth of all these thy prophets, and the Lord hath spoken evil concerning thee."

1 Kings 22:13-23

The truth of God has the absolute power to expose lies and lying spirits.

Many are thrown off by this scripture because even the prophets are affected by the lying spirit. This shows the fallibility of the vessel. The church today would be ready to cut off all prophets and today's pastors would be ready to ban the prophetic from their church. There would be lives on Facebook and Instagram concerning this occasion.

However, no matter how many prophets were affected by this lying spirit, this one principal remains true. God will always have a prophet on reserve ready to preserve His truth.

This is the type of prophet or prophetic person you must be in today's time! You must be the vessel that preserves His truth despite the trend!

Chapter Two:

God's Prophetic Church

I believe God's entire church is and should be prophetic. First, we must understand that the foundation of God's church is built upon apostles and prophets with Christ being the chief cornerstone (Ephesians 2:20). Therefore, to do away with the prophetic would require complete obliteration of the church's foundation. Some would argue that prophets nor the prophetic are needed today and they were only needed for the old testament. But Paul makes it very clear that apostles, prophets, evangelists, pastors, and teachers will be needed "*till* we all come in the unity of the faith, and of the knowledge of the Son of God, unto a perfect man, unto the measure of the stature of the fulness of Christ" (Ephesians 4:13). Anyone who says that these things have been fully accomplished, I question their sanity! "*Until we all*" is the timespan on the necessity of apostles, prophets, evangelists, pastors, and teachers.

As part of the foundation of God's church is on prophets, that means the entire makeup and attributes of His church are prophetic. *Prophetic* is defined as having the attributes of prophets or prophecy. Practically, to be prophetic means you believe God still speaks today and that His prophets are alive and active in today's time.

"For as many as are led by the Spirit of God, they are the sons of God"

Romans 8:14

This is a scripture I use very often. This is because it speaks to so many things about how God works and moves in our current dispensation. The sons of God are those that are led by His Spirit. You cannot be led by anyone that you cannot hear. How important is it to be able to hear, feel, perceive, and yield to the one that is leading you? I would dare to say extremely important!

To receive the Spirit of God means you must also receive His direction and leading. Even Jesus says that this Spirit of truth will lead into all truth (John 16:13). It is impossible to receive and believe in the Holy Spirit and yet not believe that God is still speaking today. It's almost oxymoronic.

I believe that the church should be the largest entity of God's voice for the current day. Christ made it clear He was building His church on the rock of revelation (Matthew 16:18). The church should be an agency that hosts relevant revelation for the times and seasons of the world. Beyond praise breaks, fancy fashions, and illustrious aesthetics, God's church must be full of those who bear the current heart of God for their time. The church 10 years ago is completely different from the church of today. And the church 10 years from now will be completely different from the one today. Now, the foundations will not have changed but the necessary revelation will. 10 years ago the revelation of sanctification was necessary. Today the revelation of grace is necessary. 10 years from now the revelation of kingdom advancement will be necessary for every church to stand and thrive. The attribute called prophetic is what gives the church the ability to serve the right revelation at the right time that the world needs it the most.

Company of Prophets

Before there was a set institution of the church born in the book of Acts, there was still an institution of God's voice called the company of prophets. This company of prophets was not just clusters or groups of prophets, they were known as guilds, schools, and an overall center of training and education for prophets.

The company of prophets was organized and built out with systems that contributed to its structure. Within this company, there were prophets who played instruments, there were prophets who sang, there were prophets who wrote poetry, and there were prophets who just prophesied through the spoken word (1 Samuel 10:5). This almost sounds like a "church" to me!

"And Saul sent messengers to take David: and when they saw the company of the prophets prophesying, and Samuel standing as appointed over them, the Spirit of God was upon the messengers of Saul, and they also prophesied. And when it was told Saul, he sent other messengers, and they prophesied likewise. And Saul sent messengers again the third time, and they prophesied also. Then went he also to Ramah, and came to a great well that is in Sechu: and he asked and said, Where are Samuel and David? And one said, Behold, they be at Naioth in Ramah. And he went thither to Naioth in Ramah: and the Spirit of God was upon him also, and he went on, and prophesied, until he came to Naioth in Ramah.And he stripped off his clothes also, and prophesied before Samuel in like manner, and lay down naked all that day and all that night. Wherefore they say, Is Saul also among the prophets?"

1 Samuel 19:20-24

Amid the company was a strong spirit of prophecy (1 Samuel 19). The spirit of prophecy would be so strong that it would grip the person(s) who would even enter into the proximity of the company of prophets. This is the power of the prophetic! Whether you are a prophet or not, the voice of the Lord has such an arresting capability that it can interrupt any man who comes close to it. What church would not want this within their local assembly? May men return to the desire to be completely arrested by the Spirit of God!

It was also governed by a senior prophet. Samuel and Elijah are known as two prophets who governed the company. Even with the voice of the Lord being the center and the focus, God still used man to govern and steward the institution in the earth. Let's put a pin right there! Just because you are prophetic, does not mean you are excused from submitting to authority! In fact, prophetic people must be the most submitted to Godly leadership and authority. Prophets and prophetic people risk the infiltration of pride and rebellion when their capability to hear God affects their heart of humility. Just because you are capable of hearing God does not mean you are above submitting to Godly authority. There is no prophet that God would call to only rise against and rebel against leaders – that just is not God's code of ethics for prophets and the prophetic realm.

Elijah and Samuel governed intuitions that gave God's voice a habitation in the earth. In essence, that is the entire point of God's church. God's church is more than a building or a community service opportunity, it should build "... an habitation of God through the Spirit" (Ephesians 2:22). Churches that do not build an habitation of God are simply just buildings – bricks and stone, nothing more. The voice of the Lord needs a secure place of representation. While God's voice lives in us, the church must remain full of those that it lives in. If not, it can no longer be classified as God's church.

When Jezebel was on a demonic agenda to kill all of the prophets, Obadiah was wise enough to hide 100 prophets in caves (1 Kings 18:4). Obadiah understood that if the vessels of God's voice go extinct, the time and season of the world would become darker and evil would only progress. Elijah himself slew all of the prophets of Baal at the brook, Kishon (1 Kings 18:40). If prophets die, evil lives! May there be men who will take up a burden to protect and preserve prophets and the prophetic in each dispensation!

Many days I find myself wishing the same wishful statement that Moses made, "would God that all the Lord's people were prophets" (Numbers 11:29). Not because prophets are glorified above any of the other offices that God has set in the earth, but because prophets have such unique responsibilities in God's church. We will dissect these responsibilities in each chapter but let's first highlight the responsibility I call *dress and keep*.

Dress and Keep

To ostracize and exclude prophets from the local church is to blind the eyes that protect and govern what comes into the gates of that particular church. When God put Adam in the garden of Eden, He put him there to "dress it and to keep it (Genesis 2:15). Dress it, meaning serve it. But *keep* in the Hebrew is *shamar* – meaning Adam had a responsibility to guard, protect, and defend the garden. It was Adam's mandate, as one who had been given all dominion by God, to guard the garden. In this same way, prophets have been assigned to *shamar* the gates of God's church and kingdom! Habakkuk was a prophet set as a watchman, a guard (Habbakuk 2:1).

Churches that do not establish and set prophets within their local church leave their gates defenseless! Demons and principalities that come to attempt to rule over God's church can be seen from afar when prophets are occupying the gates. Leaders who are threatened by Hell can receive a warning when prophets are seeing and interceding from the gates!

May the prophets of the living God receive their charge to *dress* and *keep* His bride!

The revival that God seeks to release within His church will be forfeited if the prophets cannot *shamar*. As prophets are voices of deliverance, fire, healing, and breakthrough, if they are silenced then the breakthroughs that are secured will only be for a moment. Israel was not just brought out of Egypt by a prophet, they were also preserved by a prophet (Hosea 12:13). Preservation comes from the prophetic. Prophets not only bring God's bride to the place of victory, but they also preserve the victories that have been won by continuing to *dress* and *keep*.

Chapter Three:

The Anti-Prophetic Church

Subsequent to the abuse of the prophetic realm, a deep disdain has infiltrated the heart of God's bride.

When some hear "prophet", their minds automatically associate the word with a bad experience they've had with someone who claimed to bear the nature and office of a prophet. This has created quite a few different ideologies that essentially sum up the idea that all prophets are after a profit or that the church today has no real ones left.

There are a few different causes that I believe, by way of spiritual understanding, have contributed to the growth of conceptions and theories against prophets and the prophetic, at large.

The Prophet Was Not a Prophet

One spiritual error that the body of Christ has seen is improper placement. Improper placement happens when we place men in categories or offices that are based on gifting and not commissioning (from God).

The scriptures show us 3 tiers, or what I like to call dimensions, of the prophetic. Spirit of prophecy, gift of prophecy, and then lastly, the office of a prophet. When teaching this principle, I teach it in the shape of a triangle.

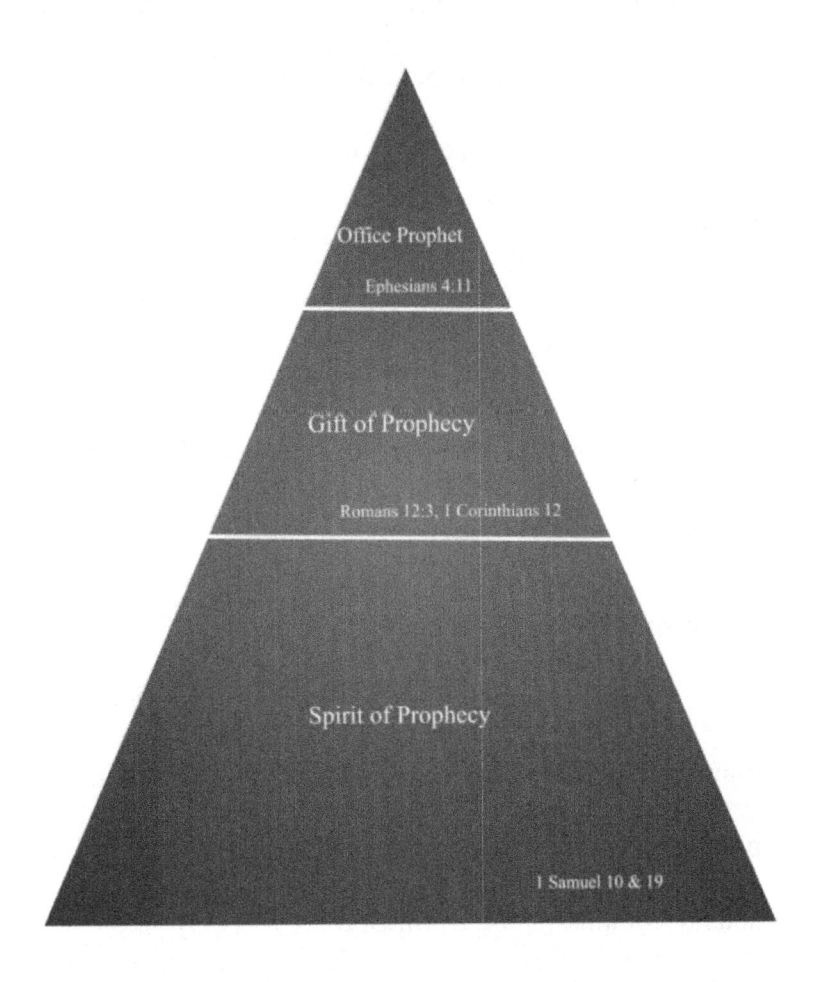

Office Prophet
Ephesians 4:11

Gift of Prophecy
Romans 12:3, 1 Corinthians 12

Spirit of Prophecy
1 Samuel 10 & 19

This triangle is to show you how largely, or minimally, available each dimension is. The spirit of prophecy is the base of the triangle and the largest part because everyone and anyone can operate in that dimension. This is shown through Saul and his messengers in 1 Samuel chapters 10 and 19. The gift of prophecy is second and slightly smaller because the gift of prophecy is only given by Holy Spirit to whomever He chooses (1 Corinthians 12). However, the office prophet is the smallest part of the triangle because it is a part of the 5 fold gifts given to men by Christ in His ascension back to Heaven. He gave **some** prophets (Ephesians 4:11). Prophets are born and are commissioned by God.

"Before I formed thee in the belly I knew thee; and before thou camest forth out of the womb I sanctified thee, and I ordained thee a prophet unto the nations."

Jeremiah 1:5

"And the spirits of the prophets are subject to the prophets."

1 Corinthians 14:32

These two scriptures give extreme insight into how God handles prophets.

1. Prophets are born

> Before Jeremiah is formed, his life is ordained as a prophet. This means that if you are not a prophet, desiring to be one is not what makes you a prophet!

2. God ordains Prophets

> Jeremiah was not ordained by a man. The fruits of his calling were confirmed by men in the earth – but his ordination service had already happened in Heaven. You cannot be

ordained by your favorite bishop as a prophet just because you or them feel like it's right.

3. Prophets have a specific spirit

The word spirit in Greek here is *pneuma*. Which means the spirit, i.e. the vital principal by which the body is animated. The rational spirit, the power by which the human being feels, thinks, decides. What does this mean? Prophets are born with a specific spirit, specially designed and created to carry out their call. The spirit of a prophet determines how a prophet thinks, walks, acts, talks, judges, etc. This is why authentic prophets can be discerned by other prophets.

Therefore, any person who has placed themselves into the office of a prophet based on a feeling or desire has been misplaced. The office of a prophet is not achieved by desire. Think about how much damage can be done when men are placed within the body of Christ as it pleases themselves and not as it pleases God (1 Corinthians 12:18). It's like taking a construction worker, putting him in a black robe and sitting him as a judge in a criminal court. Although he has a certain expertise and he very well may have some education, his skills, training, and judgment are not suitable to sit in the seat of a judiciary.

This exact thing has been done in the body of Christ. We have dressed men up, laid hands on them, and sent them out in the name of something they were not placed in by God. Your ability to prophesy does not mean you have been ordained by God as His prophet. It could very well mean that you have been given the gift of prophecy by the Holy Spirit or perhaps the spirit of prophecy was just on you for the moment like it was on Saul.

Saul prophesied when he got into the company of the prophets (see diagram for scripture). In this, people around him automatically asked "Is Saul among the prophets?" What type of damage would've been done if Saul listened to the associations of people with an office he was not being called to sit in?

The Prophet Wanted a Profit

Paul was absolutely right when he wrote "The love of money is the root of all evil" (1 Timothy 6:10). Money is not evil but the undisciplined love for it is. Avarice, or greed, does not just go after lawyers, entrepreneurs, or natural men – it goes after men and women of God too. Greed subtly enters the heart to contaminate its motives. Prophets who have been oppressed by the spirit of greed will sell out the word of the Lord for a profit, a financial gain, or benefit.

The obvious danger here is that the truth of God's counsel can never be bought with physical currency. Ergo, buying the vessel could never persuade God to change His mind.

Sowing monetary seeds into men and women of God are at the free will of any believer; however, buying or paying for prophecy is a spiritual error.

"And they came to Balaam, and said to him, Thus saith Balak the son of Zippor, Let nothing, I pray thee, hinder thee from coming unto me: For I will promote thee unto very great honour, and I will do whatsoever thou sayest unto me: come therefore, I pray thee, curse me this people."

Numbers 22:16-17

Balaam, the prophet, was seduced with honor, earthly promotion, and money with a wicked motive by the king, Balak. This king wanted Balaam, the prophet, to curse the children of Israel. To persuade the prophet, Balaak used what he thought the prophet needed. This alone shows the error of the king's ways because if you are sowing into a prophecy or a prophet's life, it needs to be done unto God, not unto an agenda of persuasion (Colossians 3:23).

If the heart of the prophet is not baptized in the absolute desire of God, anything that looks good can persuade it. A heart with a desire for honor from men can be persuaded against God's agenda, even for an authentic prophet. Prophets must let God process their hearts in every season. A vacancy in the heart can cost you your obedience to God! A desire for likes can make you sell yourself out of the truth of God's counsel.

As a child, I battled very heavily with the spirit of rejection, as most prophets do. Rejection is a demonic spirit that hides out in the conscious. The spirit of rejection will make you do things unnatural to you just to be accepted by the person or people in front of you. Before God sent me out as a prophet to nations, He intentionally dealt with the parts of me that desired acceptance from people. Being accepted is great – but being accepted at the cost of your divine obedience to God is not! It is possible to gain the world and lose your soul (Matthew 16:26). What is the benefit of having men like you but God does not? What is the benefit of men accepting you but God rejects you? The reality is being a carrier of God's truth will result in the hatred of men. Men will hate your life when it bears His unadulterated truth and His standard. Jesus warned His disciples "If the world hate you, ye know that it hated me before it hated you." (John 15:18). This does not mean that unsaved people are going to hate you. This means anyone who bears a love for the world, carnality, fleshly desires, and vain lusts will hate you – yes even if they are in church!

The prophet that lives for a profit has already lost His trust with God's secrets. God trusts men that fear Him with His secrets (Psalm 25:14). The antithesis of the fear of the Lord is the fear of man. Reverence for what man gives, thinks, or offers over God results in the automatic bankruptcy of God's realm of secrets.

Father, I pray for every reader right now. Those that are prophets will be so sold out to the will of God that no amount of money, fame, or fortune can make them go against Your will. I loose the blood of Jesus and the spirit of Your convictions to be in their heart as they serve You, Jesus! Let greed, pride, arrogance, and deception be obliterated by the Spirit of Truth today! We break and cast down the assignments of wicked intentions. In the name of Jesus, we declare all hearts are being purified today. The heart of the body of Christ be purified. The seat of the heart's desire be washed today. In Christ's name, amen!

Chapter Four:

Rise of the Real

The only way that God can expose the fake is if He raises up the real thing. Perhaps, the state of the church cannot progress into authenticity because you've been like Elijah hiding asking God to anoint someone else.

"But himself he went a day's journey into the wilderness, and came and sat down under a juniper tree: and he requested for himself that he might die; and said, It is enough; now, O Lord, take away my life; for I am not better than my fathers. And as he lay and slept under a juniper tree, behold, then an angel touched him, and said unto him, Arise and eat. And he looked, and, behold, there was a cake baken on the coals, and a cruse of water at his head. And he did eat and drink, and laid him down again. And the angel of the Lord came again the second time, and touched him, and said, Arise and eat; because the journey is too great for thee. And he arose, and did eat and drink, and went in the strength of that meat forty days and forty nights unto Horeb the mount of God. And he came thither unto a cave, and lodged there; and, behold, the word of the Lord came to him, and he said unto him, What doest thou here, Elijah? And he said, I have been very jealous for the Lord

God of hosts: for the children of Israel have forsaken thy covenant, thrown down thine altars, and slain thy prophets with the sword; and I, even I only, am left; and they seek my life, to take it away. And he said, Go forth, and stand upon the mount before the Lord. And, behold, the Lord passed by, and a great and strong wind rent the mountains, and brake in pieces the rocks before the Lord; but the Lord was not in the wind: and after the wind an earthquake; but the Lord was not in the earthquake: And after the earthquake a fire; but the Lord was not in the fire: and after the fire a still small voice. And it was so, when Elijah heard it, that he wrapped his face in his mantle, and went out, and stood in the entering in of the cave. And, behold, there came a voice unto him, and said, What doest thou here, Elijah?"

1 Kings 19:4- 13

The only way to defeat a lie is with the truth. An anti-prophetic church will believe that the only way to fix the lies of the false prophets is to eliminate all prophets. This is the deception of Hell and the furtherance of a wicked agenda!

The only way to defeat falsity is to let truth arise. When God arises (truth), His enemies are scattered (lies) (Psalms 68:1).

When the Bride of Christ lets the voices of the future, the prophets, re-establish their voices, she will see uncontrollable and consistent breakthroughs and movement. As long as Elijah sat under a juniper tree in what looks like a form of depression today, Israel would have not received its next directions, instructions, or future leaders.

You believe your obedience or disobedience only affects you. This is the problem! The longer you wallow in your rejection as a prophetic voice, you sit on the sidelines of the advancement of Satan's agenda to dishonor the authentic voice of God. A mouthful right? Exactly! God is waiting to raise you up but you are allowing fear to grip you and preclude you from releasing the truth you bear in your spirit. I declare the end of fear's intimidation on your call and your voice as a prophet or prophetic voice ends today! Get up!

There is a journey that is awaiting your ordered steps of obedience.

Prophets and Systems

God called Jeremiah a prophet to the nations. In reality, not all prophets will be sent to prophesy to nations or national leaders. However, it is important to understand that all prophets are called to affect some type of system. A government is a system that governs or sets the way of life. Nations have governments. The church is the governing agency of God in the earth but it also has a government. Some systems govern the marketplace. Let's look at how prophets can affect each. Prophets like Joseph, Samuel, and Elijah, and many others were prophets who were called to systems.

1. Nations

Nations have governments. Before nations adopted systems of man, nations were governed by God's voice. When God was governing Israel with His voice by way of the prophets, Israel complained (1 Samuel 8:4). When Israel asked for a king, it was more than just them asking for a leader that they can see. In spiritual reality, it was them opting out of God's government and requesting a system governed by a fallible man. From that moment the government of Israel struggled. Some kings obeyed God, some kings did not. Although we live in a different time and most of us are not under monarchies any longer, we see the same pattern. What is governed by man will look like man, imperfect. This is why prophets must not be afraid to arise in nations and their systems. Without God, nations fall but with Him, nations will rise (Job 12:23).

Elijah is one of the prophets who sees the rise and fall of Israel within his prophetic career. By Elijah's words, the entire nation of Israel saw no rain for 3 years. Just recently in August 2022, I visited Dallas. While in my Lyft from the airport to my hotel, my driver was telling me how the city had been affected by 30 days of no rain. People were panicking, selling their cattle, and houses were catching on fire all from one month without rain. Imagine being in the middle east without rain for 3 years. The dangers and the damages of this drought most likely affected everyone from the least to the greatest. However, by this same prophet, God uses him to release the rain (1 Kings 18). Do you think this was done because God was bored? Absolutely not! This was done so that God could prove even if you are prospering, the only one that can affect the system of nations is me!

I believe the COVID-19 pandemic was the perfect time for prophets to prove God's ability to affect the nations like Elijah did. Pandemics are the perfect opportunities to release and speak into God's plan! When destruction hits a nation, its systems are grievously affected but its ear is uniquely open to hearing what God has to say.

2. **Church systems**

Samuel was a prophet and a priest. There is a special merge between prophet and priest when the prophet is not just called to the system of the nation but also to the system of God's bride, the church. Prophets were sent from God to man, priests went to God for man. Therefore, a prophet with a priestly role is a prophet called to bring God's church into His council while also bringing God into the hearts of the people. Samuel spent his younger years ministering before the Lord in the temple with Eli (1 Samuel 3). This was not to pass time nor was it just to develop him as a prophet. Samuel's time ministering before the Lord in the temple was to acquaint him with the systems he was called to serve. In Samuel's time of ministering to the Lord, the Lord spoke to him about the state of the church while in Eli's care (1 Samuel 3:12).

Prophets called to affect the church's systems must spend a great deal developing history with God's house and His presence. These prophets spend great deals of time in prayer and prophetic intercession for God's church. They contend and defend God's bride with the perspective of God's intention for it.

I am a church kid at heart. For a long time, I felt like I was probably born in one of the pews at the church I was raised in – that's how connected I felt to church. In my younger years, I thought it was just because I loved going to church. When I grew older, I realized it wasn't a love for the "events" of church, it was a love for the church as the heartbeat of God. As a child, the only way I could interpret this love for church was through prayer (and having church throughout and around my house… imagine how annoyed all of my older siblings were). In prayer as a child, I can remember asking God to just bless the church I was at and the few churches I visited with my pastor preaching out. I can remember asking God to bless my pastor. These were my days of developing the cadence of God's heartbeat for His bride! For me to serve the church the way I do now, I had to acquaint myself with how God feels about it as an institution. I remember not really saying much other than the request for Him to bless the church and my pastor but I would still weep, and I would weep for hours. Again, I thought well maybe I'm crying because I'm sensitive for church but later I found out I was weeping because God was weeping over His bride.

Sidebar: This is why it's so important to know who your child is. If Hannah raised Samuel like a normal child, she would've kindled the anger of the Lord. If my parents would have treated me like a normal child, my destiny would've been greatly hindered and halted. I was able to enter into doors in the Spirit very early because my parents understood that they were raising God's child! Parents, please know when your child is not your own. Yes, you have been trusted to carry him or her, and the honor will be yours for doing that – but you must give that child back to God as Hannah did. Even Mary, the mother of our Savior knew the child was not her own.

Prophets called to serve the systems of the church are prophets who devote their lives to its progression and movement in God. Anna was a prophetess who spent her time praying daily in the temple. Her devotion to the temple gave her enough discernment to see the next move of God in Christ while he was still just a baby (Luke 2:36-38). These prophets give language and direction into the administrations of God, the focuses of the church and the time-sensitivity of them, they prophesy into God's agenda to build His church, and they see and warn against the gates of hell that are attempting to oppose the church.

An anti-prophetic church sabotages itself of safety and defense when it muzzles the prophets.

3. **The Marketplace**

Joseph was a dreamer of dreams but also had a keen insight into interpreting others' dreams. In Genesis 41 while Joseph is in prison, Pharaoh has a dream that even his magicians cannot interpret. When God is ready to move in a certain market or industry, the movement can only be seen by His prophets. This dream that Pharaoh has speaks to what God is going to do in the food supply. There would be 7 years of plenty in Egypt and then 7 years of famine would arise after that. From God, Joseph gives Pharaoh the answers to the time of famine that will arise. Joseph gives answers and strategies to a market that he had little if any, education or experience in. As unfortunate as Joseph's experience was from his jealous brothers to false accusations, at the hour when the prophetic was needed the most, he was able to save an entire economy.

How detrimental would it be if Joseph stayed in prison angry at God and refused to speak for Him because of the pain of his life experiences? The words in the mouths of prophets called to affect the systems of the marketplace help to navigate the seasons of plenty and the seasons of famine.

Despite what economists of the country are saying concerning the condition of the economy, prophets are needed to look and hear in the Spirit for what God wants to do in the economy. One of the things Prophet Sharon Stone mentioned by way of revelation from Holy Spirit is that the fear of the world shifted from Covid-19 to scarcity in 2022. Just like in the days of Joseph! Therefore, how do we properly prepare for a food shortage or coin shortage? We prepare by letting God reveal the strategy and direction into the voice of the prophets.

Remember the story I told of my dear friend consulting with me about his employment opportunity. The simple statement from God saying, "This is not the door" saved him time and money. In less than a year he would have been unemployed.

You must understand that God is invested in the welfare of His people. If He were not, He would not tell us to "…prosper and be in good health even as our soul prospers" (3 John 1:2). Therefore, because He is so invested, He will speak and direct us into this prosperity.

Sufferings are seasonal. When you are suffering for God financially, it is meant to be a lesson not a lifestyle! Learn to lean on the voice of the Lord for wealth strategies and economic advantages!

Perhaps immediate answers won't always be released for different markets. However, prophets called to give insight into industries must be willing to contend for the direction of the economy, harvest, and see for the famine.

One of my best friends was being threatened by her 9-5 job to be fired. She had a business in her spirit but didn't know how to break into the industry. She asked me "should I leave my job?" Again, I was pressured to hear God concerning this woman's life and financial condition. Immediately, I received a prophetic impression that her release had come. She began working on her business full time and even received some wisdom from some other prophets who were entrepreneurs. Three years later her life is fully sustained by her business.

Now, do you see why you must rise as a prophet of God? Do you see why the church needs to become the safehouse for prophets and not the institution that destroys them?

Prophets are being called by God to affect systems! Give language for what cannot be seen with the natural eye!

These are the days when there is a rise of a pure breed of authentic prophets who have been born from the loins of God. The world has seen the promotion of fallible men but now the world will see the rise of men and women who bear the heart of God in real-time. These men and women embody the full essence of what it is to be prophetic.

Before there was google, before there was a fully written Bible when men wanted to hear from God, they sought the seers (1 Samuel 9:9). I declare the revival that has come is the reviving of this concept – men will seek out the prophets that see and hear. Not the prophets who prophesy houses but don't give the strategy to get it. Not the prophets who prophesy land but don't release where and how the land will come. Authentic voices that press into the revelations of God for times and seasons will be sought out by nations, churches, and the marketplace.

Chapter Five:

Not Just Jezebel

Restoration of the prophetic and the prophet's rightful place in God's church comes when the opinion of man is completely obliterated by the word of God. Releasing the pure word of the Lord in the timing He gives makes prophecy undeniable and undebatable.

"But if all prophesy, and there come in one that believeth not, or one unlearned, he is convinced of all, he is judged of all: And thus are the secrets of his heart made manifest; and so falling down on his face he will worship God, and report that God is in you of a truth."

1 Corinthians 14:24-25

The word unlearned in this scripture lets us know that the power of true prophecy does not just affect those that are not saved, it can also affect those that just don't know. I've come to realize many people who have a disdain for prophecy often are just afraid of the change it might bring or the shift that will come as a result of its release. Ignorance is so strong that it will make you hate a thing you've never even studied. Many people within the church of God are saved but unlearned. If prophecy pricks the heart at the right time and in the right moment with the right words from God, it causes even the unlearned to bow to what they do not know before God.

Perhaps prophets have spent too much time trying to convince their pastors that they were prophets instead of just letting God give them the right opportunity at the right time to prove their fruit. An apple tree does not need to convince anyone that it's bearing apples. That is seen by all who come in contact with it. The same is for every prophet or any other calling. The tree is known by the fruit it bears. Therefore, the prophet's only responsibility is to bear the fruit at the time fruit is needed.

The prophetic is being restored in churches all over the world. A sincere honor for prophets and prophecy is being revived. It will only be advanced by the covenant of the vessel. Isaiah made a covenant to be sent (Isaiah 6). Jeremiah made a covenant to see and speak (Jeremiah 1). Elijah let God destroy his caves (1 Kings 19). As the bearer of God's council, you must hold to the vow you made when God asked you to speak for Him. And if you've not made a vow, you must today!

As the church embraces prophets again, we must war against what comes to strangle prophets and kill the prophetic word in every generation. Many prophets believe only the spirit of Jezebel is after them and it's not the only one. Let's deal with them.

1. The spirit of Jezebel

Jezebel was the evil wife of Ahab who had a wicked agenda to kill all of God's prophets to promote and elevate Baal's prophets (1 Kings 18:4). Baal is a false god who is actually still worshiped by many in deception today. Even after Jezebel was killed in 2 Kings 9, it is clear she's deposited so much evil in the earth that her spirit and legacy of evil still lives. Revelation 2:20 reveals that the church of Thyatira is letting the spirit of Jezebel teach and set herself as a false prophetess.

The spirit of Jezebel has a deep, viscous hate for prophets and the voice of God. Although Jezebel was a woman, this spirit does not operate in women alone. This spirit can be laced in entities, entire organizations, men, and any door that it can creep into. People and organizations who intentionally kill prophets with their hands or their words are operating in the vile spirit of Jezebel. Jezebel was known for her threats against Elijah (1 Kings 19). This spirit has limited authority. It may affect vulnerable prophets, but it will not affect the prophets who are confident in their calling and the safety of the One that sent them, Jesus Christ.

2. Spirit of Leviathan

Pride fights every prophet. To see and hear what others cannot since birth creates the easy plight of falling into pride. Elijah's fear of Jezebel's aggression made him run away. When he ran away, he felt justified in doing so because after all, he was the "only prophet left" (1 Kings 19:10). Whenever you think or feel like you're the only one who really has God, you've fallen into pride's trap.

Frustration a lot of times can be rooted in pride. You become frustrated because other people don't see what you see when, in reality, they aren't supposed to! I remember I had fallen into pride's trap around the year 2015. I was just really stepping into my revelation as a prophet and I became frustrated because it seemed that other people weren't on my level. PRIDE! This spirit deceives you into thinking that you're supposed to be frustrated with who you're called to. If you are the first to come into the revelation of the kingdom within your family or circle, then pioneer it with grace and humility – don't brag about you being the only one who received it. The reason why God rebuked Elijah by humbling him back into the right perspective of there being 7,000 other real prophets was because Elijah needed to be reminded – you're doing a great work, but you're not the only one! Prophets, fight pride with everything you have. To be exalted within yourself is the mistake that Lucifer wishes he never made.

3. Spirit of Divination

Divination is the enemy of the prophetic. Divination includes soothsaying, palm-reading, fortune-telling, or any other wicked entity that attempts to access the future without Christ. In Acts 16:16, a young girl made a fortune by soothsaying. The same is still happening today. People will pay psychics for a short phrase that is limited in its information. Divination in Greek is *Puthon* which actually means python. Pythons constrict and restrict to suck the life out of their victims. To constrict the word of the Lord, the spirit of python will set itself in cities and nations to intimidate men and women of God from releasing the real word of the Lord.

This spirit has a strategy. Its strategy resembles the strategy of the python snake we know and see today. The only way to defeat this spirit is to have a word sharp enough to cut through it. The word of God is the sword of the Spirit (Ephesians 6:17). Prophets without a sure word of the Lord are liable to fall into divination's trap! In every season, be full of the word of the Lord – it is the most effective weapon against this python spirit.

4. Religious spirit

Please do not think that religion is wrong. Religion is defined by Webster as the commitment or devotion to faith. In a time like today, you must be committed and devoted to your Christian faith. However, a religious spirit is a spirit that persuades a person to keep its worldly, unsaved opinion and dress it into the appearance of sanctification. A religious spirit will let you operate like the devil and transform into an inauthentic, disingenuous "appearance" of Christ (2 Corinthians 11:13-14).

This spirit is sneaky but destructible because it hides out in church but has a deep disdain for the liberty that the word of the Lord brings. This spirit will creep into the heart of the critical believers. Its main ability is to criticize what it cannot deliver or set free. Therefore, it will come with an intentional objective to eliminate prophets and anything that can release what God is saying currently. This spirit does not mind scripture-shower or sermons that have no Spirit of God in them. As long as everything has a good look but no real power of God, this spirit is satisfied.

I vividly remember being invited to preach at a particular church that I had never preached at before. Quite a few people from the church were excited because they heard my reputation as an emerging prophet at the time; however, once I arrived and met the senior pastor, I was met with an alarming prophetic impression that he did not like prophets. I did not know what to do other than obey God. In the midst of me preaching, as a prophet, I began addressing things that the body of Christ was dealing with and being challenged with at that time. While preaching, the senior pastor kept making this one comment "Oh that's not happening here". Being completely thrown off guard, I kept allowing Holy Spirit to lead me in what to say. Without specifying who was dealing with what, I kept addressing the challenges of the church at large and what God desired to do about it! If you are a prophet, you should never come with identified problems only – you should carry solutions also! In the middle of me releasing my sentence about the spirit of pride that

God was ready to deal with in His church the senior pastor whistles and says with a loud voice "You are an accuser of the brethren and that's Satan's job!" I stopped and stood in utter disbelief. The anger of my spirit yet embarrassment of my crushed feelings filled my heart simultaneously. I couldn't believe this happened in a church of about 40 people present to hear me preach.

What did this experience teach me? It taught me that a religious spirit will stop anyone from breaking through in Christ and the revelation of His kingdom. In no way would I present a church's problems or accuse someone of doing evil things but the fact that this man could use scripture to twist it towards me revealed to me the destructible nature of a religious spirit and its wicked agenda against prophets.

5.   Spirit of the Antichrist

To be against the prophetic is to be against Christ. The previous writings were meant to prove to you how invested God is in the prophetic.

This spirit of the Antichrist is the adversary of Christ. It opposes His opinion, His name, His principles, and His laws. This spirit does not even allow the entry of Christ into its environment. Do not be fooled, this spirit is not just able to operate in an unbeliever. This evil spirit can lie in the chambers of men's hearts. It lets their hands worship God while keeping their hearts from Him!

Everything that Christ does, the Antichrist does the exact opposite. If Christ releases hope, the Antichrist releases disparity. If Christ releases life, the Antichrist opposes it with death. If Christ releases a righteous decree, the Antichrist releases unrighteous decrees.

This spirit does not just operate in one. Even now, there are many Antichrists (1 John 2:18). The realms of God are opposed by this spirit. Antichrists don't just resist, they are set as Christ's opposite.

Many other demonic spirits fight prophets and resist the word of the Lord. The greatest joy out of all of this is that the word of the Lord is like a hammer that breaks rocks into many pieces (Jeremiah 23:29). I declare you will see the breakthroughs of the word of the Lord!

The purpose of identifying these spirits that operate in systems, organizations, and churches abroad is so that you will not be surprised when you are targeted by Hell. As a prophet or prophetic voice, your life becomes Satan's target. But the sword you carry is sharp enough to cut. The hammer you swing is strong enough to smite! In the name of Jesus, may your spirit never be void of the word of the Lord! May

His speaking Spirit always be in communication with your spirit.

As you journey with Christ, be the restoration of His authentic voice in the earth. Restore the power of the prophetic throughout the world. Prophesy relentlessly!

Prophetic Glossary

These words and definitions are meant to help you build your understanding and language in the prophetic. These are the definitions of the author based on the interpretation of scripture.

Discernment – the weighing and judging of matters by Holy Spirit. Discernment is used for spirits, seasons, times, places, and nations.

Gift of Prophecy - one of the 9 gifts given by Holy Spirit to whoever He chooses (1 Corinthians 12).

Novice Prophet – a prophet who has just come into his or her prophetic awakening; has not received full training and is still in the process of maturing.

Prophesy - To release God's thoughts, council, and will in the earth (the verb/action). To prophesy.

Prophet - God's messenger and spokesman in the earth. Ordained and Commissioned by God (see Jeremiah 1).

Prophetic - to believe that God still speaks today. Possessing the attributes and abilities of God's voice – may not necessarily be a prophet but has access to God's voice (spirit of prophecy, gift of prophecy)

Prophetic Burden - a word that sits on a prophet for seasons (or even years) at a time. Burdens are the weight of God's concerns.

Prophetic Career - the time of your life walking in obedience as God's prophet

Prophetic Counsel – direction, advice, wisdom given by a prophet; divinely influenced by the voice of God. This wisdom is not a wisdom based on experience. It is divine wisdom.

Prophetic Covering – the prophet's ability to hide or cover others. Obadiah hid the prophets from Jezebel's slaughter (1 Kings 18:3-4).

Prophetic Growth – growing is a natural occurrence but prophetic growth means you have grown before the Lord. Your maturing has happened in the place of God's presence and voice (1 Samuel 2:21).

Prophetic Impression - a spiritual urge felt in the senses of the prophet or prophetic person. Most times, impressions do not come with words, just a feeling.

Prophetic Incubation – the time that God calls the prophet into hiding (cave). This incubation is not meant to last forever; it is ordained by God and its seasons are determined by God.

Prophetic Intercession - prayers made on behalf of another (an individual, God's church, nations, etc) infused with the voice of God's will. These are not prayers of one's heart's desires. These are prayers laced with God's desire for another.

Prophetic Interruptions – seasons of darkness or evil are the perfect seasons that God chooses to birth prophets. Samuel's birth was an interruption to no open vision in Israel in 400 years. Elijah was the perfect interruption to the reign of Jezebel's evil.

Prophetic Warfare – the warfare of prophets. Prophets and prophetic people have an advantage in spiritual warfare. They don't just fight demons and principalities aimlessly. They fight demons and principalities from the direction of

God's voice, making it clear what to target. This type of warfare carries another level of precision.

Prophetic Wealth – The wealth that God gives. It is strictly supernatural. It is not worked for nor merited; it is given by God. "Wealth which God shall give Israel" (1 Samuel 2:32).

Senior Prophets/ Prophetic Seniority – Obadiah addresses Elijah as lord (1 Kings 18:7). Senior prophets are those who have been trained, developed, and matured by God; reaching a place of governing authority.

Spirit of Prophecy - the testimony of Jesus (Revelation 19:11). An atmosphere created by worship and the presence of Jesus – this atmosphere stimulates God's voice and anyone (even unsaved) can hear and release the voice of God within this atmosphere.

Word of Knowledge – a gift of the Spirit. Information about someone or something that is divinely given by God to an individual.

Word of Wisdom – a gift of the Spirit. Wisdom or guidance that is divinely given by God to an individual. Holy suggestions made from God.

About the Author

Prophet Darius K. Walton is an apostolic and prophetic leader burning with the passion of revival. Called to be a pioneer within his era, Prophet Darius Walton has unashamedly carried out the charge and mandate to call the body of Christ back to the heart of God by way of prayer. As an author of 3 books, <u>Prayer Still Prevails</u>, <u>Devoted to Demonstrate</u>, and <u>Like An Ox</u>, he maintains his commitment to prayer and demonstrating God's kingdom and the power thereof.

Undoubtedly, the hand of the Lord has been upon Prophet Walton's life from before he was placed in his mother's womb. Through his obedience to God, Prophet Darius Walton has seen masses come in contact with the authentic, supernatural power of God through accurate prophetic ministry, deliverance and healing ministry, and fervent prayer.

Prophet Darius Walton serves faithfully and humbly as the senior leader of Demonstrate Culture located in Wilmington, Delaware. Demonstrate Culture is not just a local church but also is a multigenerational and multicultural global movement.

Prophet lives by his favorite scripture - Proverbs 19:21, "Many plans are in a man's mind, but it is the Lord's purpose for him that will stand."